LITTLE MILLION DOORS

AN ELEGY

WINNER OF THE NIGHTBOAT POETRY PRIZE

LITTLE MILLION DOORS

AN ELEGY

CHAD SWEENEY

NIGHTBOAT BOOKS
NEW YORK

ISBN: 978-1-64362-000-8

Design and typesetting by Margaret Tedesco
Text set in Frontage and Palatino Linotype

Cataloging-in-publication data is available
from the Library of Congress

Nightboat Books
New York
www.nightboat.org

for my father
Everett John Sweeney
1945–2010

LITTLE MILLION DOORS

My skin felt heavy I left it
Draped

Over a chair to walk out

Cross the wet
Colors of may I could

See time glow I could

See the ancestors
Of trees let me

Ask you this

What name was I each

House in a
Street of houses my

Hands in the trees for bells

I promise to what
Purpose was my story the

Ripple of snake

Skins or sounds long
In the curtains

Long days of rain a phone was ringing

High over the steps the wet

Gables of the world immortal it was

Our souls streaming into quiets

Of woodgrain toward what

Plane of convergence for years I could not

Answer a music in pain the undying

Will undying in the dying grass

And the road was all
Of bones

And all and only I
Was on it

Walking to where at noon forever

A voice
Far and thinly

Filling up
The canyons the boxes

Of its meanings
I say *was*

What I mean is
Will be

I tried to peel away the names
I said who is god

And watched the sound

Ripple into green
I tried to pray said take me

To the center spread thin I was
Everywhere if

Cities

Are nothing a single bucket
Of night is enough

My clothes grew tired an
End of day I begged this

Air to
Hundred me

As many genders
As bees

In the lavender field my
Lovely hero

What nothing like sleep did the water
Where have you

Gone little murder find me here

Did I grow a shadow in this did I belong

To table and to roses
A woman

Leads
The skeleton of a dog

Her mouth floats by praying

Beneath her eyes where time
Gusts

Against the slow
Hills and where

Am I in this the hills
Are listening

See me I almost shout

Or I do shout I must be

Like green day stars a few

Washed out in the low heaven

I am the heaven

That touches to shoelaces to
Steps the white

Lamps still lit at noon I enter

The museum to color
Square spaces of paint

With my absence

Is
This memory I am watching

A girl in red

Wool leads the sheep a long
Line of them over snow

And they follow her small as
She is is

This my country
Inside the animals an

Empty larger than the
Falling in the falling

Of the snow

The grass is gold and white
The dead lawn of the courthouse

The moon

Shaking the statues
Are white the moon

Radiant throwing its rings out
Pins the shadows

Of dying animals old
Coats

Cut from the sleep of mares

The elms slow
Poplars gather the dark

To spin it out

Against a grave in the moon's
Fire

I stood up from the pit
From the pits the air

Was busy with us

All of us it was
Faith only in

Gravity held
An agreement one swallow

Flew up from zero a signal

Fire seen one
Mountain to the next

Carried by deer a living
Shadow on the wall I hear

The valley hurry over to relive

Weathers of other lives
I am born I bear the cry

Each animal its word in breaking
Seven nested futures who

Were we
Heaps of bones making love I

Storm
In shells of color past pouring

Out from if
Threads of inert

Fire
Trace the boundaries of a wheel

Are these the shapes
I loved I

Study the faces from inside them
In trains looking out

Over fountains
From inside them the ivy

Over bridges is this happiness
From inside them the clover

In the statues in the shaking
Of butterflies

A tattoo my daughter's

Name in
The garden I remember

My daughter in the high
Collective

Well of summer
Is necessary for something

To watch stars begin
A gust of stars between

The skull and skin and moving
Out to find a rib is it

Mine to lie beside a hundred
Years this wide

Reflective face of water is there
No shape for grief

The now what if

Petals blow the stems
I remember!   Daisies   Daisies

In a word against the west
Wall of the house

I was murdered I was
Stillborn I died old

I tried on these robes in

Light reposed over patterns
Of water

Surrounded then traced
All futures brimmed

Under grapevines
The wind a flower I relived

My death
Or someone's

Here
Language opens at the wound

Here the house
Of effects

Its procession of

Candles inside the body
One long day the body

A lantern how
To say it

It it

Lantern in a window
Is the body hundreds

Of panes
Into sorrow moving

Beneath the river road

I've tried to hold
To anger a snow

Delineates the thin
Winter

Branches

But I am a tree of no branches
Tree of no tree

If I let it
The snow

Throughing me down

In
Pieces tiny with it

To drifts
All of me and blue

To lie up long
Underside bridges

To feel the life
Pass over

In wheels in warmly
The stories each heart's dark mouth

Saying yes and saying yes

To pretend to fall to pretend

To be afraid whimper give me

Bone to shelter
The weight of it even

A rope the last yellow
Night

Stirs the bluebells this hill
I would carry my heart

On a pillow yes
To lie down

I would carry my body
All the way back

I would carry
The eyes of it I would

Carry the hands of it
I would wash

The skin I would
Bear the feet I would draw

The blood out long and shine it

And there are too many moons
Each of us

Through prisms
Echo the brightly

Against columns the columns

A bodiless animal
Eating the air

Above tracks
Where no train is

Little million

Doors and darkly
From here the future

Looks like many attempts to ask

There are gods but not the ones
I thought there are

No gods the story

Turns
Under me the hooves

Of me leave on yellow sheets

Of rain
Over the awnings

I am allowed

Nearer
To foxes and to eggs

Of sparrows in the
Open I

Map my finger to sheer

Vertical air to
Ask direction in fire alone

Has no memory of this
Morning my nerves stretch

Along highways
To form a clock is there

Nothing outside me to remain
Still among the possibles

A single light

Death it could be asked
Innumerable
Shadows inside me
Whatever the opposite of lightning
Hangs

Unbearably above the barley field

And I was carrying my blood to a
Height above the city
And dropping
It but nothing like a shout
Fell from me a
Whole just then
Into shining

From every
Where a well in air

Into infants the names give

At the transom the women
The men no season

Only dahlias today
Falling one long day

The invisible city a wind
Of causes

The flocks of me
Multi

Ply in brambles in
Pastures the cars

Into rye the woodlight of
Tables our silence

Surrounds us with surfaces

Outside myself I remember
A hill carrying

Water up and all
Of us

As bowls of water he
She

Carries up to jasmine
I raise

My fists the bees
Like a mask I'm shouting

But what I hear
For the dead I hear waves

Against the sun roaring nothing

Is what I thought

Only outlines visible

In gold thread a chair
A bell I think

What the tipping

Coppers of leaves in green shade
Is swaying the lines

In the face
Of what breaks in gravity

The small below a swing

Or one cat I think long

Time in the window

Ago squared
Where no wall is

The real

Doorframes in wind the blood's radiant
Green flower

And scarves tangling
Among all the blond

Grasses one
Chickadee gathered the day

Into smallness
The dunes and the dunes

And the water

Hills farther out in waves

A distance to watch me
In the intricate

Deliberations

Of selves I know iron

Grasses the flocks of geese
Arrows returning to surfaces

Of what I am lying into
The ground and up through

Planes of sky its people

In lines through the air
Is a miracle

Inside me the canyons
Intimate if ravines a

Current

Of bear and one red
Branch I touch my

Water
The ripple the root of it here

Is thought is memory

Gathers in
Woodgrain the seasons to come I

Watch

Myself inside myself in
Side myself

To plant the eyes in
Side my eyes

In the dark a dark I bear
My ladder of one

Rung the quiet
Within a hammer

The white sleeve
Of a window

Is mine an inch of
Air or

Children
On the bus to listen

Inside them each heart
Like a cardinal

In its thicket

What is it to live
Is to want to live

A pearl translucent what

The rivers are burning
Air in columns is everywhere

Burning the fields of phlox
In spaces

Of office and morgue snow
What lights

The rooftops the rooftops
I am looking but there is no

Me to do the looking
Between branches between bars

In prisons I was framed
By doors the dusk

Of the body was no where
And the whole sea

Or a wide rain fell
Over cornfields and over roads

Over the blue
Disc of the mountain the

Wind the east wind
Tuned the rain was all teeth

My few teeth only repeating

The days I lived my task to
Gather them

Some
Days days in halls

Of hospitals the court
Rooms places of dying

I only

Hear language
In shells

Of insects water
In water

The mouths open to need

The words clear
In jades in whites

From the eyes I think

Nets and sway
Above the capitol

Come words

Or they are rushing away

Crossing bogs under
Doors somewhere far

From themselves into moths
If pollen a weather

Carries above tobacco
Fields they suspect none of this

Is human the bricks the moon

Their fingernails and blood
An empty no mother

Behind curtains of water

Abyss in the shape
Of a maple leaf

Leaf to be in two
Eras at once scaffolding

Under the hill the other
Sun a river

Boat and its story

Painless I abide
Traceries of bees slide over

To say soul the world is

This all we are
A soulfield in sound we

Adrift in
Sleeves

I could almost
Sleep it

A series of blue doors

The days come floating
Away from me

Inside stone a wind
My daughter

Horizons in the wood
Her bouquet in

Ruins

At both ends
Of the road

Where nothing needs
Saving

Or someone's shadow
Working

Like a hammer
Shadow of a thought

Working high

Above the water wheel

Delicate the boy
Swaddles

A babe across the mine field
Innocent the gravity in

Ropes singing down

The whole earth like a
Mirror for something

Where helicopter blades
Flower

Three in the low sun

At bottom of the
Street like a well

Into deeps
The street where

Looking
Time trebles in the smoke

Of cedar groves the dogs
Drift

Into us a shout the cold

Into us a little while
Light lets nothing is

Sovereign a page a box
Brimming

All delicate
In the body held

In the coarse
Rope netting

Of the body time keeps

Branching what

Does it want in us each
Carries her

Death like a vase of deaths
Was I

Married in the soft sleep

Of marrow I can't explain
Children see me

Inside them I watch
Language move the year

They don't know it's over
For a while

In museums
In circles the public

Fountains
They follow someone a few

Steps is he mine am I that
Until no one it's

Quiet they float up
To hang

Their feet in magnolias
All ripple and thinly

Until they are many
Feet in many trees the slowing

Of light
Is a new kind of everywhere body

Death I think if there is such a
Place in beauty

Landscape
Without the landscape in it

And nothing outside me
Thin colorless

Sky among the olive
Branches and in the long windows

Of children's mouths
My life without me in it at the center

Of no center is a flower

At the wedding
Of the air the man

Exhaled I gazed him
Close up the skull

Of him glowing
Like a window what

Passed between us had many
Blue threads the children

All of mirrors the planet turned

Away over sand and testing

Bombs I let myself
Want something

My life stared
Where it wasn't

This smoke which is
The fine smolder

Of thought shines clean shines
Dirty no matter

Onto the road
The road carries

Leaves away to where
Swiftly

We may not follow
We leave our arms on shelves

Or the small child of us I try

The clocks to zero
No matter watching gamblers

The dice of them each

Outcome true to love
The wars they killeachother

They put antlers on fences
Don't eat

My shadow not one bite
They put

Fires on ledges this is
My shadow three hundred

Eggs the sun lay my voice

Moves beyond me across
The water has

Lost its way I am bound

To watch murder in the old
Country a girl

Sold for her heart

Its million red bells
Help me

On a pillow yes I would
Place the voice I would

Wear the lungs
To which orders of musics

Have I belonged
To ships to valleys the thought of me dilates

An iris yes in
Ripples of mustard

Field and trash heap
Lets

Crows by crowlight into milk
Which

Language is this shaping the coffins
A white heat

Adumbrates the sycamores the
Houses I think inside

The wake where I am not

Alone in faith
If there is anything

Only time which has

Been blowing

White over the red

Hills red

Over the bronze scoring

The windows of thin

Ivory the fires

Gone out the cities

Piled with antlers

The orchards sub

Tracting apples and waves

Under bridges as monuments

Of granite one may walk across

The delicate hinge of no

Fulcrum

Is what it meant

Or someone's hipbone wears the whole
Night this tender sequence

Above the market

Holding very
And very still

To keep
To a glass chair in the river I

Magine a temple
Surrounded by itself

Is another word for wind

I was quickling
Through archways

Over grainfloors and water the arches were only
My body the wet

Steps of libraries
Room after room the fountains

A page of air I was
Looking for an end

In the book of everything
In shafts

The miners in salt
Marshes a turtle's

Wet roof in
Reeds and mud and watching

Thistle release its down
Where hold and release

Were one word in the small I was

Futuring the thistle to twelve
Distances of

God what is this between us a world

A man there is follows
Me

Through woods every age but this

Is no woods ahead on the road
The hands

Flutter
Windows whole rooms of his body

In doorways his voice in
The crossing who my

Son in cedars is he
Me from the bell note

This thunder under
Granite understands us

To occupy the turnings

Of sky below the river
No difference between seeing

And hearing
Returned to the rim of zero

Begging upward into stairs
The hands

Follow me
Into the sun

What am I
That shakes

The mountain's high tree is
Generating distance

Sending it out in waves
Against the air

What happened
Between us I remember the

Future a white branch
Of water split into

Gathering into its tree
One drop of blood at the mouth

Of the delta this altar

Waiting for me
A weather my footsteps how

In all
Directions surrounding then

Fleeing
To carry

A boy was measuring the day
He had a big hoop

The sun emptied its arrows

Into him
He thought the hoop invisible

I wanted to tell him

Inside those
Arrows oh thankly and final

Not much of me left

And this must be what love

Feels like this
Spreading out over

Surfaces

Of leaves they flicker out

The children they are all
Children now their hands

On the drums the borders and
Bread is and is

This the gift

INDEX

ACKNOWLEDGMENTS

Deep gratitude to the editors of the following journals in which sections of *Little Million Doors* first appeared: *Colorado Review, Denver Qtly, VOLT, Omniverse, From the Fishouse, Josephine Quarterly, Mead: the Magazine of Literature and Libations,* and *The Account: A Journal of Poetry, Prose, & Thought.* I would also like to express my gratitude to poets who have read and supported this work: William Olsen, Nancy Eimers, Jennifer Kochanek Sweeney, Suzanne Parker, Juan Delgado, Julie Sophia Paegle, Nikia Chaney, Scott Bade, Traci Brimhall, Elizabyth A. Hiscox, Douglas S. Jones, Gary McDowell, Laura Donnelly, and certainly Kazim Ali, Stephen Motika, Lindsey Boldt, Margaret Tedesco, and all the luminous people at Nightboat.

Chad Sweeney is the author of five previous books of poetry, *Parable of Hide and Seek*, *White Martini of the Apocalypse*, *Wolf's Milk*, *An Architecture*, and *Arranging the Blaze*, and two books of translation, *The Art of Stepping Through Time*, the selected poems of Iranian dissident poet H.E. Sayeh (from Farsi with Mojdeh Marashi), and Pablo Neruda's final book, *Calling on the Destruction of Nixon and the Advancement of the Chilean Revolution*. Sweeney's poems have been included in *Best American Poetry*, *The Pushcart Prize Anthology*, and *Verse Daily*. He is the editor of the anthology *Days I Moved Through Ordinary Sounds: Teaching Artists of WritersCorps in Poetry and Prose* and Iroquois elder Maurice Kenny's posthumous collection of poetry and prose: *Monahsetah, Resistance, and Other Markings on Turtle's Back*. Sweeney holds an MFA from San Francisco State University and a PhD from Western Michigan University. He is an Associate Professor of English/Creative Writing at California State University San Bernardino where he edits *Ghost Town Lit Mag*. He lives in southern California with his partner, Jennifer Kochanek Sweeney, and their two little boys.

NIGHTBOAT BOOKS

Nightboat Books, a nonprofit organization, seeks to develop audiences for writers whose work resists convention and transcends boundaries. We publish books rich with poignancy, intelligence, and risk. Please visit nightboat.org, to learn about our titles and how you can support our future publications.

The following individuals have supported the publication of this book. We thank them for their generosity and commitment to the mission of Nightboat Books:

Kazim Ali
Anonymous
Jean C. Ballantyne
Photios Giovanis
Amanda Greenberger
Anne Marie Macari
Elizabeth Motika
Benjamin Taylor
Jerrie Whitfield & Richard Motika

Nightboat Books gratefully acknowledges support from the Topanga Fund, which is dedicated to promoting the arts and literature of California.